DRINKING
games

AND hangover cures

fun for the BIG
NIGHT OUT and help for
the MORNING AFTER

mark vale

DOG 'n' BONE

This edition published in 2023 by Dog 'n' Bone Books
An imprint of Ryland Peters & Small Ltd.

20–21 Jockey's Fields   341 E 116th St
London WC1R 4BW   New York, NY 10029

www.rylandpeters.com

First published in 2015

10 9 8 7 6 5 4 3 2 1

A CIP catalog record for this book is available from
the Library of Congress and the British Library.

ISBN: 978-1-912983-67-4

Printed in China

Designer: Ashley Western
Illustration: Artworks from The Games chapter
by Kuo Kang Chen, except for pages 5 (top right),
18 (bottom left), 25, and 29. All other illustration
by Stephen Dew

Contents

Introduction 11

THE GAMES

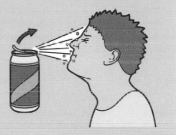

THE CURES

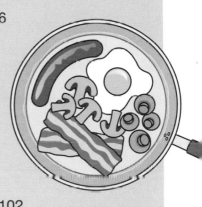

DISCLAIMER:

The author and publisher disclaim any warranty or guarantee, express or implied, for any of the instructions, or anecdotal information, contained in this book. They further disclaim any liability for the reader's experiments, or damages that may occur as a result of reading or following any of the material in this book. The application of information offered is at the reader's discretion and is their sole responsibility. The purchase of this book by the reader will serve as an acknowledgment of this disclaimer and an agreement not to hold the author and publisher responsible for any problem, injuries, or misdemeanors that may occur indirectly or directly from the use of this book.

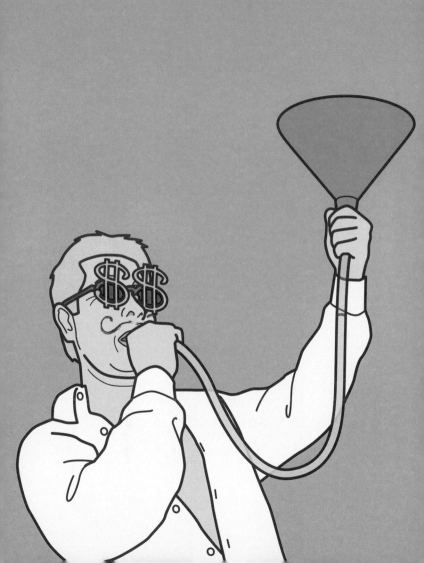

Introduction

Calling all booze hounds, bantersaurs, party animals, beer monsters, mega lads, and cocktail lovers, put down those drinks and pay attention. You have in your possession a powerful tool in the quest for alcohol-induced nirvana, use it wisely.

After years of extensive research and exhaustive testing, all in the name of science of course, we are proud to present our findings: 25 of the most awesome drinking games in history. From challenges to play with a friend or two,* to ones certain to bring any party to life, every game will result in an unforgettable night of booze-fueled fun.

But here's the rub: when you embark on a round of drinking games, unless you're blessed with the constitution of Oliver Reed or a member of the Rat Pack there's a very good chance you're going to be feeling just a tiny bit fragile when you wake up the next morning. Don't panic, because we've also done our homework on how to get you up on your feet

*Never play drinking games on your own—that's just weird!

in record time. With innovative cures from around the world, you will easily be able to beat that drilling in your skull and stop the churning sensation in your stomach that indicates you will soon be talking to God on the big white telephone. Aren't we good to you?

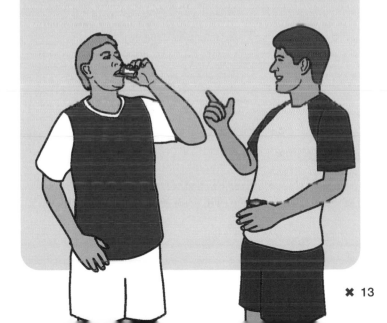

A Friendly Piece of Advice

When it comes to hangover cures, a little bit of forward planning goes a long way. It is recommended that you pick the cure (or cures) that you'd like to try the next day well in advance of your drinking session. Some of the ingredients can be slightly tricky to come by and, as far as we're aware, a hangover cure delivery service doesn't exist (but it should, that's an ace idea!). So, be sure to buy all the required elements ready for when you need them most.

The
Games

Let's Play!

Drinking games have been around as long as there's been drinking. In fact, it's highly likely Neanderthals used to sit around their caves on

winter evenings and pass the time by goading each other into munching on tons of fermented fruit.

Fortunately, nowadays, we don't have to rely on half-rotten apples to get our kicks. And after eons of ritual drinking, we've developed some classic games to ease the passage of booze down our throats. This book brings together the best of those classic games, plus many rather unusual ones.

Forfeits

Most drinking games require players to complete a task. Failure in that task results in a drinking forfeit. The strength of this forfeit should depend on the constitution of the players. There's no point making each forfeit three shots of vodka, unless you want the evening to end especially quickly.

Easy forfeits might be a finger of beer (i.e. a slug of beer equivalent to the thickness of your finger against the side of the glass). Dangerous forfeits might be large shots of liquor or whole glasses of beer. Drinking games normally work best if they feature lots of little drinks over a long evening.

Tough luck if you happen to have very fat fingers.

Beer Hunter

👥 **Players:** two to six

🍺 **Equipment:** a six-pack of beer

➕ **Hangover potential:** two

🏃 **Skill:** zero

Remember that scary scene in the 1970s Vietnam War film, *The Deer Hunter*, when Robert De Niro and Christopher Walken are forced to play Russian roulette in a Viet Cong prison camp? Well, this is almost as extreme, except you replace guns with cans of beer, and enemy soldiers with your drinking comrades. Oh, and play it outside if you don't want to ruin the carpet.

Place a six-pack of beer on the table. Shake up one of the cans extra vigorously and shuffle it up among the other cans so that no player knows which has been shaken. Each player then chooses a can, holds it right up close to his or her face, and pulls the tab. One player ends up being doused with beer, while the other five emerge unscathed.

As additional punishment, the player fresh from the beer shower has to down an extra can of beer.

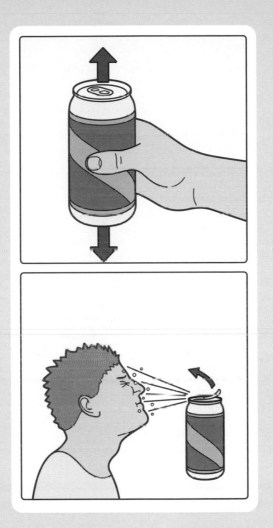

Blind Barman

Players: three or more

Equipment: pack of cards and a well-stocked bar

Hangover potential: four

Skill: one

Ever struggle to create the perfect cocktail? With this game you can throw caution to the wind since you'll end up mixing some of the most revolting concoctions known to man.

Line up as many liquors and mixers on the table as you can possibly find. Next, lay a pack of cards face down on the table. Each player takes turns picking up a card. The first one to pick up a king gets to choose the liquor. The second king chooses the mixer. Then—yes, you guessed it—the third king gets to down the impromptu cocktail. Just like it's been mixed by a blind barman.

Whisky and tomato juice, anyone? How about a delicious mix of crème de menthe and pineapple? To really spice things up, include the two jokers in the pack. Pick those up and you have to drink a double dose.

Last Card

👥 **Players:** two or more

🍷 **Equipment:** a pack or cards and a bottle of wine

➕ **Hangover potential:** three

🏃 **Skill:** four

This game is designed to test both your drinking prowess and your coordination.

Place a full pack of cards on top of a wine bottle. Players then take turns in putting their mouth up close to the pack of cards and trying to blow just a few of the cards off the top of the pack. Whoever ends up blowing the final card off the bottle has to down a glass of wine.

Of course, it's all about finding a happy middle ground. Blow too softly and it could take 52 blows before the drinker is finally allocated. Blow too hard and you'll tumble the entire pack straight away. Of course, the fun part is that the more you drink, the harder it is to blow with any degree of accuracy.

Liquid Legends

Booze and firearms never mix. Unless you're in the British army, that is. Apparently, a favorite drinking game involves two officers, a bike, a shotgun, some light shot, and a bottle of port. The two protagonists start off by flipping a coin. The loser immediately jumps on the bike and pedals off as fast as possible, while the winner necks the port, loads the gun, and tries to shoot his opponent in the back.

Flip, Sip, or Strip

👫 **Players:** three or more

🍺 **Equipment:** a coin and a full set of clothes

➕ **Hangover potential:** three

🏃 **Skill:** one

This is the ultimate ice-breaker since it involves both drinking and stripping.

Sit in a circle. Each player takes turn flipping a coin. Guess heads or tails correctly and you pass the coin clockwise for someone else to flip. Guess wrong, however, and you have two options: either drink or remove an item of clothing.

Most players spend the first half of the game going for the drinking option. Then, as inebriation sets in, they spend the second half on the stripping option. Much like an average evening in a bar, then.

Ozzy Osbourne

👫 **Players:** three or more

🍺 **Equipment:** a good knowledge of famous people

➕ **Hangover potential:** three

🏃 **Skill:** four

Like all the best games, this one is deceptively easy to start off with, but rapidly becomes very tricky. Sit in a circle and allocate a player to start. All he or she has to do is state the name of someone famous. Any celebrity will do, real or fictitious, from pop star to politician, actor to astronaut, just as long as other players have heard of them.

The next player has just five seconds to name another famous person whose first name begins with first letter of the last name of the previous celebrity. So, James Bond might beget Britney Spears. Britney Spears might beget Saddam Hussein—now there's a scary thought! The game carries on in a clockwise direction unless someone says a name that's alliterative—such as Ozzy Osbourne or Tina Turner—in which case you switch directions and the player who went previously has to go again.

Fail to say a name within five seconds, and you drink. Fabricate a name or get it wrong (other players can challenge you), and you drink. Repeat a name that's already been said, and—yes—it's time to drink. It's surprising how quickly you run out of memorable celebrities to use.

Liquid Legends

One of the biggest boozing celebrities of all time was actor Oliver Reed. He once claimed to have drunk over 100 pints of beer in two days before marrying his second wife Josephine. Reed died in 1999 after a night of hard drinking and arm wrestling.

Ice-cube Tray

Players: two or more

Equipment: an ice-cube tray and a coin

Hangover potential: three

Skill: four

There comes a time in every evening when all the ice runs out. It's no good sitting there, staring at the refrigerator, willing it to freeze more ice cubes. You can put that ice cube tray to much better use by playing this drinking game.

Place the tray (one with between 10 and 14 cubes works well) in front of you on the table. You now have to bounce a coin off the table and into the tray. Keep bouncing until you successfully land the coin inside one of the sections. If it lands on the left-hand column of the tray, you can nominate someone else to drink. Land one in the right-hand column and you must drink yourself. The number of finger measures to be drunk are determined by how far into the tray the coin lands: the cube nearest to you means one finger measure; the second cube means two finger measures; and so on, right up to a maximum of seven.

Buzz Fizz

Players: three or more

Equipment: a mathematics degree

Hangover potential: three

Skill: five

If mathematics is your weak subject, avoid this game like the plague. Poor mathematicians are even poorer when there's booze on board.

Sit in a circle and take turns counting upwards from one. (So far, even a math reject can handle it.) Things start to get tricky when you reach five, however. The rule is that any number divisible by five, or that contains a five, must be replaced by the word "buzz." Likewise, any number divisible by seven, or that contains a seven, is replaced by the word "fizz." Miss a buzz or a fizz and you have to drink. (And watch out for numbers that are divisible by both five and seven, or which contain both a five and a seven. They must be called out as "buzz fizz" or "fizz buzz.")

Apparently this game is very popular with university mathematics students. There's an urban legend that a bunch of geeks once reached well over 1,000 before someone made a mistake. Mere mortals will do well to get past 100.

Liquid Legends

Ancient Greeks used to play a drinking game called kottabus. Players would yell out the name of the woman they loved while throwing the last remaining drops of wine from their cup into a metal bowl in the middle of the floor. If the drops landed right in the bowl, then a promising love affair was on the cards. If they missed, then it meant the goddess of love had rejected them.

Liquid Legends

Ancient Viking King Håkon took his country's Christmas celebrations very seriously. All his subjects were forced to drink ale throughout the entire holiday. Those who refused were fined.

Marlboro Man

Players: three or more

Equipment: a pack of smokes

Hangover potential: three

Skill: four

Smokers are so anti-social, what with nipping outside every 10 minutes for a crafty smoke. This game will ensure they remain in the thick of the action.

The idea is to take turns throwing a packet of cigarettes over your beer glass and onto the table. Land the packet on its largest surface and you immediately drink. But land it on its side, or its end, and the person next to you must drink one or three finger measures respectively. The only way he or she can avoid this is by again throwing the packet onto its side or end, in which case the forfeit increases incrementally and is passed onto the third player. Should the packet land flat at any time, then that player has to drink the accumulated forfeit.

Skilled cigarette-packet throwers can very quickly accumulate a massive forfeit for their opponents.

Edward Ciderhands

Players: two or more

Equipment: bottles of cider and duct tape

Hangover potential: four

Skill: one

There's no bailing out of this game halfway through. You're fully committed until every last drop of liquid has been drunk.

Everyone needs two large-ish bottles of cider (you could also use beer bottles, or even wine bottles for a game of Amy Winehands) and an enormous roll of duct tape. Get someone to strap an open bottle of cider to each of your hands using the tape. (It's about now that you suddenly realize why the game's called Edward Ciderhands.) Once everyone's fully taped up, you then embark on a drinking game. Pretty much any game will do, as long as it doesn't require hands— Buzz Fizz (page 36), Ozzy Osbourne (page 32), or perhaps Roxanne (page 47) would all work well. The only extra rule is that you can't remove the taped bottles until they're both empty. Not even to go to the bathroom.

Rumor has it Johnny Depp loves this game. Plays it with his buddies every week.

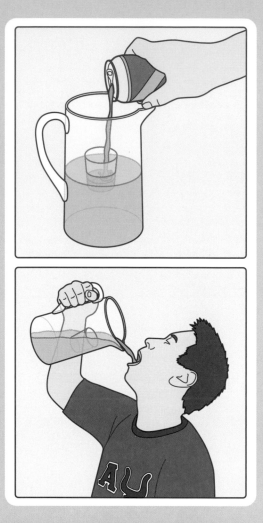

Battleships

Players: two or more

Equipment: beers, a tumbler, and a beer pitcher

Hangover potential: four

Skill: three

A favorite of frat parties, this one. And a great way to get soaked in beer if you pour too fast.

Fill a pitcher halfway up with beer. Then place a small tumbler glass inside it so that it floats upright. (You may have to pour a little beer inside the tumbler to stop it capsizing straight away.) Now players take turns pouring beer from their own glasses into the tumbler. Whoever sinks the glass has to drink the entire contents of the pitcher.

While you have to be wary not to fill the glass up too much when it comes to your turn, at the same time you need to fill it up just enough so that you don't end up running the gauntlet a second time.

James Bond

Players: two or more

Equipment: a TV/computer screen and a Bond movie

Hangover potential: four

Skill: two

The perfect drinking game for couch potatoes. Simply mix up a huge round of vodka martinis, download a Bond movie (any one will do), and sit back and wait for the fun to begin.

The rules are fairly simple, and you can adapt them according to everyone's ability to hold their liquor. Every time someone dies, you all take a sip; easy if you're watching the rather sedate *Dr. No*, but tricky if you have a high-body-count movie such as *You Only Live Twice*—91 deaths, last time we checked. The same goes for vehicle explosions and any time 007 is mentioned.

It's up to you and your friends to decide on other forfeits. You might suggest compulsory drinking every time Bond flirts with Miss Moneypenny; or every time he delivers a punch; or when he appears in a tuxedo. The options are endless.

There are two scenarios, however, when your martini must be drained right to the bottom of the glass. That's whenever the immortal line: "The name's Bond… James Bond" is uttered. Or whenever Bond orders a vodka martini "shaken, not stirred."

The genius of this game is that you can adapt it to any movie franchise you like—*Star Wars*, *Harry Potter*, *Batman*, *Rocky*, *Toy Story*. Just change the forfeits to suit. Be warned, the body count in *Toy Story* is disappointingly low.

Roxanne

Players: two or more

Equipment: a compilation album of The Police and a music player

Hangover potential: three

Skill: one

Singing and drinking have always gone hand in hand, but this 1978 song by The Police involves more drinking than you quite bargain for. To play, just stick The Police's *Greatest Hits* on the stereo, and key up "Roxanne."

There's one rule: every time the band sings "Roxanne," you have to take a big sip. Of course, it all starts out rather easy, as the famous lady of the night's name comes up just once every three lines. But, like all the best drinking games, the pressure builds up exponentially. First, the chorus kicks in, then after a short reprise for the second verse, you have the final coda, during which Roxanne's name is repeated ad infinitum.

Be warned. In all, there are well over 25 Roxannes to contend with in just over three minutes. So, it might be best to put the vodka bottle down and stick to beer or wine.

Sports Bar

Players: four or more

Equipment: a TV

Hangover potential: four

Skill: one

The trouble with watching sports on TV is that it gets in the way of good drinking time. The answer, of course, is to combine the two. And the best thing is that you can play this game with any sport, from baseball or football to tennis or tiddlywinks. Just make sure you agree the rules before you start.

Split the group into two teams, and allocate a sports team to each drinking team. Now decide on the forfeits. For example, if you're watching soccer on TV, you may have to down a shot every time there's a corner kick, free kick, or a throw-in. Triple measures every time your team scores a goal. With baseball it might be a shot for every strikeout, and a triple shot for catches and home runs.

Trust me, this will liven up even the most boring sports. Just don't choose test cricket. The drinking game ends only when the sports game is over. With cricket you could be playing for days, and even after all that the final result might be a draw.

Liquid Legends

Impress your friends. Learn how to say "Cheers" in unusual languages: Kippis (Finland); Sláinte (Irish Gaelic); Kanpai (Japanese); Serefe (Turkish); Budmo (Ukrainian); Prieka (Latvian); Prost (German).

Boat Race

Players: multiples of two

Equipment: pint glasses

Hangover potential: three

Skill: three

Ivy Leaguers and Oxford and Cambridge University students particularly love this game. Split everyone into two equal teams. Ideally, if you want to remain true to the sport, there should be four or eight on each team. Now each team sits down on the floor, in a line, as if they're all rowers in two boats. Everyone has a full pint of beer in their hand. To spice things up, place yourselves boy-girl-boy-girl with your legs around the person in front of you.

On the word "Go," the bowman, at the front of the boat, starts to neck his beer. As soon as he's downed it all, he places the empty glass on top of his head, at which point the rower behind him embarks on her pint. The game continues in the same shipshape fashion until both strokes, at the back of each boat, have downed their pints. Each member of the losing team has to down an extra pint as a forfeit.

Chicken Feed

Players: multiples of two plus one umpire

Equipment: a long table and two packs of cards

Hangover potential: three

Skill: two

This has to be the most chaotic drinking game there is. It's certainly not for the faint-hearted. You might even call it a blood sport!

Split up into two teams, with each team on the opposite side of a long table. One person—the one who is least fond of contact sports is a good choice—volunteers to be umpire.

Now scatter one pack of cards, all face up, randomly across the table. The other pack goes to the umpire who proceeds to read out, one by one, each card in his or her pack. Every time the umpire names a card, all the players quickly scan the table to locate the same card in their own pack. Then, using just one finger on one hand, they attempt to drag that particular card off their side of the table while opposing players try to do the very same thing. If they succeed, everyone on the opposing team has to drink. With 52 cards to get through, the game gets rather feisty toward the latter stages.

It's not difficult to imagine the carnage that ensues, which is why the umpire must insist on some strict rules. To win the card, the team must drag only the correct card off the table each time—more than one card and it's declared null.

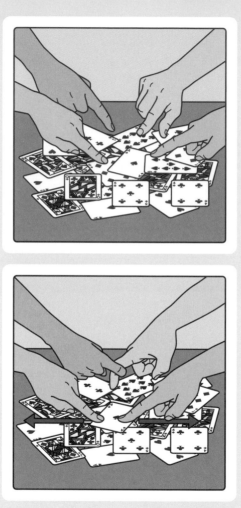

Chicken Feed cont.

Only one finger on one hand can be used. Players are allowed to use their finger to hook an opposing player's finger off the card.

Watch out for players with sharp fingernails!

Liquid Legends

Alexander the Great was one of history's most prodigious drinkers. He once organized an Olympic Games to honor a dead Indian religious leader. However, since the Indians weren't familiar with Greek sport, he opted for a wine-drinking contest instead. 41 contestants died during the Games, and the winner lived just four days after his victory.

Bar Golf

Players: four or more

Equipment: lots of bars in close proximity

Hangover potential: five

Skill: one

This classic bar-crawl game involves either a nine-hole or 18-hole course, depending on your group's capacity and stamina. Nine holes, of course, means nine different bars have to be visited. 18 holes means 18 different bars.

Assign a team captain before you start. It's his or her job to choose the type of drink for each bar. A friendly word of warning: if you're gunning for 18 holes, you may want to stick to beer! In each bar (or hole), all players must attempt to down their drinks in as few gulps as possible. Scoring is the same as in real golf: fewer gulps mean a higher score. The winner is the player with the least number of swigs by the end of the round.

To make the game more realistic, insist that everyone dresses in extra loud golfing attire: plus fours, Argyll sweaters, caps, gloves—the whole nine yards.

Beer Pong with paddles

👫 **Players:** multiples of two

🍺 **Equipment:** glasses, paddles, and ping pong balls

➕ **Hangover potential:** two

🏃 **Skill:** four

This could be an Olympic sport one day. Well, if synchronized swimming qualifies, why not this game?

If playing with two players, take your positions at either end of a table tennis table. Place three half-full, but large, glasses of beer on your side of the table. Put them anywhere you like, but not next to the net. Now start playing table tennis, but, instead of winning points, you attempt to hit the ping pong ball into your opponent's glasses. Clip one of the glasses with the ball and he or she has to down a finger measure. Land the ball right in the glass and the glass has to be drained. Whichever player ends up with three empty glasses first has to drain all the remaining beer on the table. And don't worry if you don't have a table tennis table. Any large rectangular table will work; just fashion a makeshift net out of something— hockey sticks and broom handles will usually do the trick.

This game works as singles, doubles, triples... anything that's a multiple of two. For larger games the same rules apply, the difference being that once the first team member has played a shot the rest of the teammates follow until a glass is hit. To make the game more interesting, add more glasses to the table.

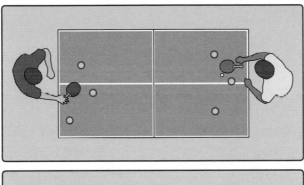

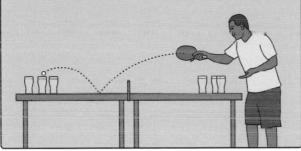

Beer Pong
hands-only version

Players: multiples of two

Equipment: at least 12 plastic cups, ping pong balls, and a large table

Hangover potential: four

Skill: five

Even if you don't have a table tennis table, you can play this game on any large table.

Start by positioning three cups at each end of the table. In front of these place another two, then one more to make a triangle shape. Fill each of the cups on your side with beer apart from one; save this for a delectable concoction of your choice... Baileys and lime juice perhaps? Repeat on the other side.

Now divide your friends into two sides and gather each team at opposite ends of the table. A member of the first team starts the game by attempting to throw a ball into one of the cups at the opposite end of the table.

This can be done in two ways: either by bouncing the ball onto the table and into a cup or by throwing it in an arc. When the ball lands in the cup, a player on the opposing team must down the contents and remove it from the table.

The second team now has the chance to return the favor and the game carries on until one side has hit the target on all the cups. The losing team has to down all the cups left on the

Beer Pong cont.

winners' side, plus an extra drink of the victors' choice.

There are a lot of local variations of this game—for example, some players add an extra row or two of cups, whilst others allow you to swat the ball away if it bounces on their side of the table. Try experimenting with your own rules and forfeits.

Coin Football

Players: two

Equipment: a square or rectangular table and a coin

Hangover potential: four

Skill: four

Stand at either end of the table. Place the coin so it overlaps the edge of your end of the table. Then, using your finger to flick, move the coin across the table toward your opponent's edge.

You have three flicks or fewer to get the coin to overlap his end of the table. Touchdown! Fail, and you drink. Succeed, and you must walk round to your competitor's side of the table, flick the coin from its overlapping position up into the air, and

Coin Football cont.

catch it. Again, drink if you fail; proceed if you succeed.

Let's presume you succeed. Now return to your side of
the table and, using two fingers, spin the coin hard on the
table surface. Before it stops spinning, attempt to trap it
between your two thumbs. Once again, drink if you fail; proceed
if you succeed.

The final section of the game is the field goal. Your
opponent makes the shape of goalposts with his hands on his
side of the table. You, meanwhile, use the thumbs you've just
trapped the coin with to flick the coin over the posts. Fail and
you drink again. Succeed and your opponent has to down his
entire drink.

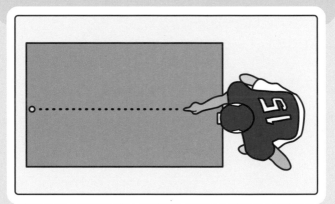

Liquid Legends

Early Anglo-Saxons often used to drink out of vessels made of cattle horns. The idea was that they couldn't be put down until they were completely empty.

Monkeys

Players: as many as possible

Equipment: lots of furniture

Hangover potential: three

Skill: one

You know those cold, winter evenings when everyone settles down for a nice, quiet drink in front of the fire? Well, this game is definitely not for fans of those kind of nights.

It's best played in a large group, while drinking at a busy bar. Without warning, one of the group will yell out "Monkeys!" at the top of his or her voice, at which point everyone must immediately avoid touching the ground. They can jump up on the bar, kneel on a chair, or leap onto a table—anywhere, in fact, as long as no part of their body is touching the ground. The last person to achieve the monkey position has to drain a drink. This player then has the privilege of being the next person to shout out "Monkeys!"

The game's even better played outdoors at barbecues.

Ring of Fire

Players: four or more

Equipment: a pack of cards

Hangover potential: five

Skill: one

Randomly scatter a pack of cards face down on the table. Players now take turns to pick up a card with the following consequences:

2, 3, or 4: The player downs the appropriate finger measures of booze.

5: Last player to raise a hand for a high five has to drink.

6: Last player to place a thumb on the table has to drink.

7: The player to the left has to drink.

8: The player to the right has to drink.

9: The player opposite you has to drink.

10: The player nominates a victim to drink.

Jack: All the boys have to drink.

Queen: All the girls have to drink.

King: The player has to drain his or her drink.

Ace: Everyone has to drain their drinks.

Feel free to modify the rules, or up the ante, as you see fit.

Liquid Legends

Humans have been making alcoholic drinks for at least the last 9,000 years. In northern China, archaeologists have found pottery jars containing the remnants of fermented rice, honey, grapes, and hawthorn berries.

Nut Race

👥 **Players:** two or more

🍺 **Equipment:** beer glasses and a bag of nuts

➕ **Hangover potential:** three

🏃 **Skill:** one

Didn't your mother always warn you not to drink on an empty stomach? While this drinking game hardly fills you up, it does actually involve solids as well as liquids.

Each player holds a peanut eight inches above his or her full glass of beer and drops it in at exactly the same time. At first the peanut sinks to the bottom of the glass, as you'd expect. But within a few seconds—hey presto!—it starts to rise. The player whose peanut resurfaces last has to down a glass of beer and munch the peanut.

Make sure you use a whole peanut. Half peanuts will sink without trace.

Arrows of Death

Players: three or more

Equipment: darts and a dart board, plus shot glasses

Hangover potential: four

Skill: five

A dart board throws up all sorts of possibilities when it comes to drinking games, but the best ones tend to be the simplest.

For Arrows of Death, each player is allocated a number on the dart board and a shot glass. Taking turns, the players then attempt to throw a dart into their number section, downing a shot each time they are successful. If they hit the double ring, they down two shots; the treble ring, and it's three shots. Play continues until all the players have downed 10 shots.

But hold on. As ever, there are a few cheeky little rules which might bring out a player's vindictive streak. If you hit someone else's number, he or she has to down an extra shot as a forfeit. Doubles and trebles increase this forfeit. Should you miss the board altogether, your forfeit is to down an extra shot. Hit the outer bull and you can nominate someone to drink an extra shot. Hit the bull's eye and everyone has to down an extra shot.

Ever wondered why professional darts players are so fat? Here's your answer: copious amounts of booze.

Liquid Legends

Lots of beer can kill you, whether you actually drink it or not, as this cautionary tale reveals. In 1814, at the Meux & Company Brewery, in London, a huge vat of beer split open, causing a domino effect which ruptured all the other vats alongside it. In the resulting flood, 323,000 gallons of beer gushed onto the London streets, killing eight people in nearby basement homes.

Liquid Legends

The Scots have always had a reputation for being big drinkers. Little surprise then that, on remote Scottish islands, archaeologists have found Neolithic 30-gallon jars containing fermented barley and oats, but with a few extra hallucinogenic treats thrown in, such as deadly nightshade and hemlock.

Who Am I?

Players: three or more

Equipment: pens and Post-it notes or rolling papers

Hangover potential: four

Skill: four

Everyone writes the name of a celebrity, either real or a fictitious character, on a Post-it note or a cigarette rolling paper. They then stick the paper onto the forehead of the player to their left so that everyone can see the name except for the person wearing it.

Each player now tries to discover the identity of his or her celebrity by asking the other players questions — for example, "Am I a man? Am I an actor?" etc. However, answers are restricted to "yes" or "no." Every time there's a "no" answer, the questioner has to drink a finger measure. As soon as they guess their celebrity correctly, everyone else has to down their drinks.

Wine Checkers

👥 **Players:** two

🍺 **Equipment:** 24 shot glasses and a checkers board

➕ **Hangover potential:** four

🏃 **Skill:** three

There's an old adage among drinkers: stick to the same color wine and you'll avoid a hangover. Of course, that rule stops applying once you start consuming bacchanalian quantities of wine, but it's a good adage all the same.

For this game of two players, you need to choose whether red or white wine is your tipple. Fill up 12 shot glasses with white wine and 12 with red. Now use the checkers board for a regular game of checkers with just two slight rule changes: substitute the checkers for the shot glasses and every time you jump a shot glass, your opponent has to drink it.

Should you manage to crown one of your shot glasses king, swap it for a larger glass and fill it up with extra wine.

Be prepared for a very sticky checkers board, and a very messy game of checkers.

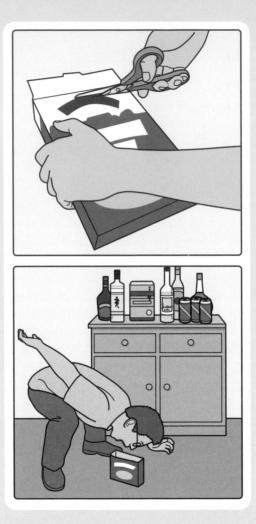

Cereal Killer

Players: four or more

Equipment: an empty cereal packet and a pair of scissors

Hangover potential: three

Skill: two

You know that Caribbean favorite, limbo dancing? This is the drinking-game equivalent. Crank up the music, stretch your limbs, and get ready to party.

Start off by placing a large, empty cereal box on the floor. Players now take it in turns to pick up the box with just their mouth. The problem is they're not allowed to touch the floor with any part of their body except their feet. (Usual drink forfeits apply, see page 22.) The other problem is that after each successful oral pick-up, a section must be sliced off the top of the cereal box, so it gradually gets shorter and shorter after each turn. Carry on playing until all you're left with is a shallow box just a couple of inches off the floor.

It won't be long before the drinking forfeits are coming thick and fast.

Blind Relay

Players: multiples of two

Equipment: beer bottles, a large table, and two blindfolds

Hangover potential: three

Skill: two

This is just like the 4x100 meter relay race, except you're all blind, and, if you play it long enough, blind drunk.

Split into two teams. Place several opened bottles of beer on a table at the far end of the room. Players now take turns negotiating their leg of the relay. This involves wearing a blindfold and being spun around 10 times before running across the room. When they reach the table they must grab a bottle of beer and down it as quickly as possible before running back to their team. The relay continues until all players have downed a beer and successfully navigated their way back to the start.

The losing team has to drink any remaining beers.

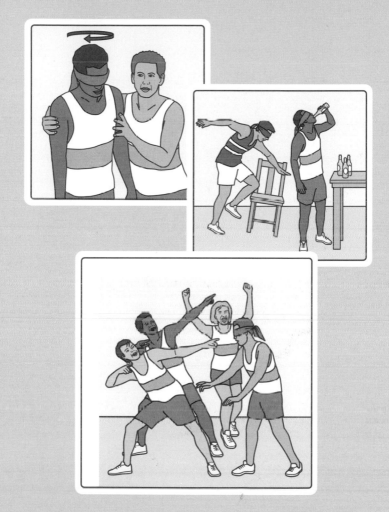

The
Cures

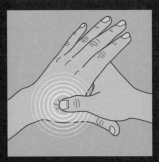

A Note on Hangovers

Here's the bad news: there's no guaranteed cure for a hangover. After a long night of seriously irresponsible boozing, it's unfortunately inevitable that you'll have at least a brief visit from Mr. Headache, Mrs. Nausea, and their unbearable kids Dizziness, Dehydration, and Stomach Upset.

However, the good news is that your house guests don't need to hang around all day. There are many different ways to ease the symptoms of excessive drinking. In this book you'll discover all sorts of remedies, ranging from alternative medicine, food recipes, and drinks (both hair of the dog and virgin) to activities, pharmaceuticals, and old wives' tales.

So what exactly happens to your body when the hangover kicks in? Alcohol contains toxins which arc distributed round your body via the bloodstream. As your liver breaks down this alcohol, it creates a rather nasty substance called acetaldchyde. In small amounts, this is okay, but drink too much and it builds up in the body, causing nausea and headaches.

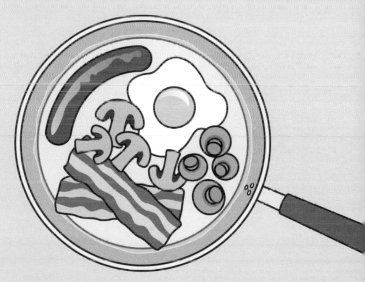

The headaches are made even worse by alcohol's diuretic effect. For every drink you down, you expel four times as much in urine, dehydrating you massively. As the water is drawn away from your brain, these headaches get worse because the brain shrinks, pulling on the membranes that attach it to the skull. No wonder it feels like a skunk has crawled into your head and died overnight.

All this is exacerbated by a poor night's sleep. Alcohol causes your body to produce less of the natural stimulant glutamine. Once

you stop drinking, your body then goes into glutamine overdrive, making you toss and turn all night.

But enough of the science stuff. The reason you're reading this book is because you have a monumental hangover. You don't want to waste what few brain cells you have left worrying about acetaldehyde and glutamine. What you need is a remedy. Take your pick from the very best we have selected.

The Water Remedy

✔ **Lots of isotonic sports drink**

✔ **A prison shower or ice-cold mountain lake**

You need to rehydrate, and rehydrate fast. Isotonic sports drinks are best for this. They contain salts and sugars similar in concentration to those found naturally in the body.

While you're putting water back into your insides, it's a good idea to give your outsides a similar treatment. However terrible you feel the morning after, a cold shower will blow away the cobwebs. Just don't bend down for the soap. (No, really. By leaning over, the body will pump more blood to your brain and your headache will get even worse.)

Even better than a cold shower is full-body immersion. What about a dip in the ocean or an ice-cold mountain lake?

Liquid Legends

Had Harry Potter been a boozer, he might have favored this witchcraft hangover remedy. It involves brewing tea from the shrub damiana, a plant that according to Mexican folklore was used in the original recipe for margarita cocktails. Apparently, it's also an aphrodisiac. Watch out, Hermione!

The Sauna

- ✔ **A sauna**
- ✔ **Lots of drinking water**
- ✔ **Twigs and snow (optional)**

When it comes to the sauna, it's the Scandinavians who know best. There's many a time the effects of a Stockholm all-nighter have been alleviated by a morning spent naked in the hot box. The idea being that the heat draws the toxins of the alcohol from your body.

You have to take a few precautions, however. Saunas, of course, draw even more fluid out of your body than the drinking session already has, so neck lots of water both before and after. Also, be warned: some medical experts believe alcohol and extreme heat can lead to irregular heartbeats and, in extreme cases, cardiac arrest, so don't stay in too long.

In Finland, a sauna often includes a spot of gentle slapping with twigs to encourage the skin pores to open up. This is followed by a quick roll in the snow to close the pores afterwards. There's no evidence that either activity will do much to combat your hangover, but, hey, it will certainly take your mind off your headache. Especially if there are a group of naked Finns in the sauna with you.

Coconut Water

✔ **Several coconuts**

✔ **A mallet**

There's no complicated science behind this one. Again, it's a simple case of rehydration. Coconut water—extracted from the nut when it's still too young to form milk—contains pretty much the same electrolytes found in the human body.

A mark of its efficacy is that it's occasionally been used in hospitals as an intravenous drip when conventional fluids have run out.

And, recently, it's become so popular that commercial drink manufacturers have jumped onto the bandwagon. One concoction, known as VitaCoco, has even managed to secure Madonna as an investor.

Coconut Water

The BLT

- ✔ Four rashers of back bacon
- ✔ Chunky bread
- ✔ Leaves of lettuce
- ✔ A tomato
- ✔ Mayonnaise, ketchup, and butter

Sometimes comfort food is the only answer. And you don't get more comfortable than a bacon sandwich topped with fresh lettuce and a few slices of tomato.

Even the scientists agree this little beauty can help with hangovers. A study at a British university discovered that the protein in bacon replaces essential amino acids lost during binge drinking, while substances in the pork called amines top up the neurotransmitters depleted by the alcohol.

The other bonus is that a BLT is easy to prepare, even when you're stumbling about the kitchen in a post-alcohol fog. Start by grilling the bacon until it's crispy. Slap it between two pieces of buttered toast, add some crispy leaves of lettuce, a couple of slices of tomato, a squirt of ketchup, and lots of mayonnaise.

Oxygen

If you've ever been on a skiing trip you'll know just how quickly your après-ski hangover evaporates once you hit that first run the following morning. That's all down to the oxygen in the fresh, mountain air.

Although it's not been scientifically proven, the theory is that extra oxygen speeds up your metabolism and helps your internal organs process the toxins from alcohol more quickly.

But most of us live down at sea level. We don't have the luxury of fresh, mountain air. Rush-hour fumes are about the best we can hope for during the morning after. So what's the answer? Buy pure oxygen in a can. Many companies now sell the product. You simply inhale.

Liquid Legends

Was Genghis Khan a heavy drinker? You bet your herd of yaks he was. Nothing like a good booze-up after killing 40 million people. Although history doesn't show what his usual tipple was, it's highly likely this Mongolian favorite was his hangover cure: pickled sheep's eye and tomato juice. Some Mongolians still swear by it today.

Cabbage Soup

✔ Two onions, sliced

✔ One tablespoon butter

✔ Seven cups (1.7 liters) vegetable stock

✔ Half a head of cabbage

✔ One can chopped tomatoes

✔ One tablespoon cider vinegar

✔ Two carrots, chopped

✔ One turnip, cubed

✔ One potato, peeled and cubed

✔ Salt, pepper, and chopped parsley to season

Cabbage has been a hangover remedy as far back as ancient Greece. One of the by-products of alcohol are toxins called cogeners, and cabbage helps eradicate these naughty little fellows.

The best way to ingest the stuff the morning after the night before is in soup form. And you can't go wrong with the famous Russian cabbage soup. The Russians have always been inventive when it comes to cabbages. Not surprising, really, when you think how many long winters they've had to perfect their recipes.

Their anti-hangover soup is simple to prepare and will soothe both headaches and nausea. Fry the onions in the butter until tender. Add the stock, cabbage, tomatoes, and

vinegar. Heat until it boils. Now reduce the heat and simmer uncovered for 30 minutes. Add the carrots, turnip, and potato and simmer for a further 15 minutes. Season with salt, pepper, and parsley. Be prepared for the ensuing monstrous flatulence.

Guinness and Oysters

 A pint of Guinness

 Half a dozen oysters

The Irish swear by it. (But then they swear by a lot of things. In fact, they swear whenever humanly possible.)

The only problem is, if you're Irish and you have a hangover, it's highly likely you spent the previous evening consuming pints of the black stuff. This means it will take an iron constitution to bring yourself to put more inside your suffering body the morning after. Especially if you accompany it with oysters.

There is, however, some clever science behind the remedy. The Guinness acts in a hair-of-the-dog capacity, and also includes many essential nutrients. The oysters are believed to have a restorative effect thanks to their high levels of protein.

Liquid Legends

Pliny the Elder was no fool. After all, it was this wise ancient Roman who penned the world's first encyclopedia. He was also a staunch advocate of raw owls' eggs as an effective hangover cure.

Fernet

✔ **One measure of Fernet Branca**

✔ **One measure of sweet vermouth**

✔ **Three measures of gin**

✔ **One cocktail cherry**

No one's quite sure of the exact ingredients in the liquor known as Fernet. It's all a bit of a myth. It definitely contains aloe, myrrh, chamomile, cardamom, and saffron. But, in Argentina—where it is normally mixed with cola and considered almost a national drink—there are rumors it also involves a bit of wormwood, coca leaf, codeine, mushroom, gentian, quinine, ginseng, and St. John's wort.

Depending on which doctors you talk to, Fernet can treat cholera, baby colic, menstrual pain, stomach upsets, and, most importantly, hangovers.

The trouble is, it tastes like cheap mouthwash on its own. The best way to consume it is in a cocktail. Try this lovely little number, using the most renowned Fernet liquor, Fernet Branca. Simply mix the Fernet, vermouth, and gin with ice and strain into a cocktail glass. Add a cocktail cherry for a bit of token vitamin C.

The Full Monty

- ✔ Bacon
- ✔ Sausages
- ✔ Eggs
- ✔ Tomatoes, halved
- ✔ Mushrooms, halved
- ✔ Bread and butter
- ✔ Baked beans
- ✔ Cup of tea with milk and sugar
- ✔ Black pudding (optional)

Other countries mock the British contribution to world cuisine. "Chips with everything," they say with a sneer. But there's one UK dish that silences every critic, and that's the full English breakfast, aka The Full Monty.

It may be a heart attack waiting to happen, but it delivers the perfect combination of protein, carbohydrate, and fat (plus the cysteine in the eggs) that every hangover victim needs. There's even a dose of Vitamin C in the form of the fried tomato.

Preparation is both easy and greasy. Grab the largest frying pan you can find, add a glug of vegetable oil, and fry all the ingredients together—except the baked beans, which you simply heat up in a separate pan. Serve with fried bread,

buttered toast, and steaming cups of tea. If you're feeling adventurous you can even include black pudding. (That's congealed pig's blood served in a pig's intestine, in case you're asking. And they wonder where the bad food rep comes from.)

Bloody Mary

- ✔ Five measures of tomato juice
- ✔ A freshly squeezed lemon
- ✔ A generous measure of vodka
- ✔ Worcestershire sauce and Tabasco
- ✔ Celery salt and black pepper
- ✔ A stick of celery and lots of ice

Who exactly was Bloody Mary? Some say the drink is named after the English Queen Mary. Others claim it was the Hollywood silent-film actress Mary Pickford. There are even suggestions it was a waitress in a Chicago bar called the Bucket of Blood.

Whoever the elusive Mary was, she has inspired one of the most famous hangover remedies of all time. First invented in the 1920s and championed by the likes of Ernest Hemingway, this infamous cocktail has soothed countless hangovers over the years. And it's pretty obvious how it works. The vodka acts as a hard-core hair of the dog, and the tomato juice injects some essential vitamin C.

Always prepare this drink with something of a flourish since it's really the only acceptable way to get drunk at breakfast. Fill up a highball glass with ice cubes, pour in the tomato juice, squeeze in the lemon juice, and then top it up with vodka. Add a dash of Worcestershire sauce and Tabasco

to taste, plus a pinch of celery salt and black pepper, before stirring and garnishing with a celery stick. (For a Virgin Mary, follow the same recipe, but leave out the vodka. And shame on you!)

Reflexology

With all hangovers, it's your stomach and your head that need the most attention. Reflexology—which involves applying pressure to key energy points on the body—offers two quick cures for these aching areas.

Start with the head. Using the thumb and forefinger of one hand, pinch the tender spot between the base knuckles of the forefinger and thumb on your opposite hand. Take deep breaths and hold for 30-second intervals until your headache subsides.

Now for the stomach. Apply pressure with one finger to the second toe of each foot. You're looking for the stomach meridian point—the energy highway that leads directly to your stomach. It's the point just at the tip of the toe nail of the second toe, slightly toward your big toe. Use your finger to push down on this meridian spot with a circular motion. Do this for two minutes in a clockwise direction, then two minutes counter-clockwise.

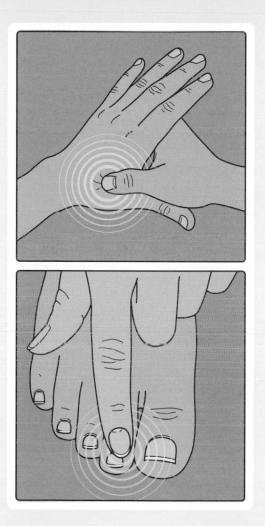

Aromatherapy

✔ **Peppermint, lemon, fennel, and juniper essential oils**

✔ **A hot bath**

Wake up the morning after a big session on the booze and there will be one overriding aroma in your nose. That's the delightful stink of alcohol seeping through your pores.

This smell obviously isn't therapeutic in the slightest. For aromatherapy, what you need are some essential oils. Since aromatherapy is not an exact science, the jury is out on which essential oils you need specifically, but many experts agree that peppermint (which cures nausea and upset stomachs), lemon, fennel, and juniper (all of which help liver function) are good options to consider.

To cure your hangover, run a hot bath, add a few drops of the essential oils into the water, and give yourself a long, relaxing soak. Breathe deeply to inhale the vapors into your lungs.

Prairie Oyster

✔ **One egg**

✔ **Worcestershire sauce and Tabasco**

✔ **Salt and pepper**

Eggs and pepper sauce have been comforting penitent drinkers for centuries. A substance in the eggs called cysteine mops up many of alcohol's toxins.

One of the best versions of this classic recipe is the prairie oyster. Break a fresh egg into a glass—keeping the yolk whole—and add a splash of Worcestershire sauce and Tabasco, plus a sprinkling of salt and pepper. Hold your breath and down it in one. As you feel it slide down your neck, you'll soon realise why it's called an oyster.

P.G. Wodehouse's famous butler Jeeves was a big fan of raw eggs and hot sauce after a rough night. In fact, the morning they first ever met, Jeeves' initial service to his new master was to mix him up a variant of the prairie oyster.

However, the original prairie oyster—favored by cowboys on the prairies of North America— featured very different ingredients indeed. Instead of the raw egg, they opted for fried bull's testicles.

Here's a bit of free advice: stick with the egg version.

Ginger Tea

- ✔ **Fresh ginger root**
- ✔ **Water**
- ✔ **Honey and lemon juice**

You'll know if you've ever had it. That mother of all hangovers where you feel so sick that you're reluctant to put anything back into your body, even fresh air. This is when you need ginger tea. It's been scientifically proven to cure nausea.

Be sure to make the tea fresh. Peel and slice up a small section of ginger root. Add the slices to boiling water and simmer for 15 minutes. Strain into a mug, adding honey and fresh lemon juice to taste.

In the Democratic Republic of the Congo, ginger is mixed with the sap of the mango tree to make something called tangawisi juice. They say it cures hangovers… and pretty much everything else you could imagine.

Brisk Bike Ride (or Sex)

✔ **A bicycle, sexual partner, or both**

Wake up after drinking your body weight in booze and the last thing you feel like doing is jogging round the park. But vigorous exercise will definitely help your hangover. It increases the circulation of blood around your body, encouraging your organs to process the alcohol toxins much faster.

Just make sure you choose an activity where you don't shake things up too much. Cycling is a good one since you're essentially sitting down, yet you can still get your heart and lungs working hard. And when you freewheel down the hills, the fresh air will give you an oxygen hit (see page 98).

What if your bike's got a flat tire, though? A gentle roll between the sheets with your other half might just do the trick. (Perhaps gentle is the wrong word, in reality the more vigorous the sex the better.) The exercise will not only help you physically, but also mentally (provided you are both in a fit state to put in a decent performance!), making your hangover a thing of the past.

Artichokes

As far back as Roman times, heavy drinkers (and, funnily enough, artichoke farmers) have constantly been championing the globe artichoke as a hangover cure. However, modern scientific research suggests it might all be quackery.

Nevertheless, the plant does have positive effects on liver function, which speeds up the removal of alcohol toxins from the body. It also helps to calm nausea.

But before you start munching your way through raw artichokes, it's worth noting that you'd need to consume dozens to get any benefit. A better option is to buy one of the over-the-counter globe artichoke extracts available in pharmacies, saving you both time, money, and the headache of where to get hold of a mountain of 50 artichokes in preparation for the morning after a night on the booze.

Yoga

✔ **A yoga mat**

Both spiritually and physically relaxing, yoga is the type of exercise you can achieve even when you're sick as a dog. The yoga move perhaps best for hangover victims is a seated twist, which works on the organs in your lower abdomen. The theory is that the twisting motion helps your liver process the alcohol toxins, which should reduce your hungover suffering.

Sit down on the floor with your legs stretched out in front of you. Pull your left leg toward your chest and cross it over your right thigh. Breathe in, sit up tall, and then twist your torso round to the left as you breathe out. Then round to the right. Now swap legs so that your right leg is crossed over your left thigh.

Be warned, though. Yoga sends energy around the body and relaxes your muscles (yes, all of them), so it often causes flatulence. If you've been on the beer the night before, you may want to practice your twists in the privacy of your own home. Farting in front of strangers is never a good move.

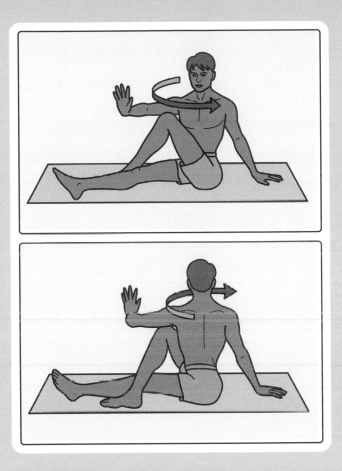

Elvis Sandwich

✔ **One ripe banana**

✔ **Two slices of white bread**

✔ **Two tablespoons of smooth peanut butter**

✔ **Two tablespoons of butter**

✔ **Two rashers of bacon (optional)**

No one gobbled up the peanut butter and banana sandwiches quite like The King. Which is why this hangover-numbing sandwich will always be known as the Elvis.

Like all the best remedies, it's easy to prepare. Mash the banana, toast the bread, and grace one slice with the peanut butter, the other with the mashed banana. Once you've connected both sides of the sandwich, fry your creation in the butter until both sides are golden brown. If you are feeling particularly rough, try adding one of Elvis' favorite ingredients to the mix: bacon. Apparently that's how his mother used to make them for him.

Before you stuff your face, pop on a white leather rhinestone suit and call your heart surgeon.

French Child's Breakfast

✔ **Croissants**

✔ **One jar of chocolate spread**

✔ **One mug of milk**

✔ **Cocoa powder (check packet for amount needed to make one mug)**

✔ **A view of the Eiffel Tower from your kitchen window**

Walk into any family home, anywhere in France, at 8am, and chances are your nostrils will be filled with the gorgeous smell of freshly baked croissants, steaming hot chocolate, and Nutella chocolate spread.

From a very early age, French kids are encouraged to overdose on chocolate at breakfast time. Perhaps it's because their parents know they face a lifelong love affair with wine. Whatever the reason, there's no doubting the restorative effects of the full-butter croissants and *beaucoup de chocolat*.

Heat the croissants for a few minutes in the oven. Heat the milk in a saucepan (the French use UHT milk), and add it to the cocoa powder, mixing vigorously. When the croissants are warm, remove them from the oven and smear them with chocolate spread. Nutella is the Frenchies' favorite.

Liquid Legends

The worst hangover in history? That award may well go to a 37-year-old Scotsman who went to hospital after suffering four weeks of non-stop headaches and blurry vision. It turned out he'd been on a four-day binge session during which he'd necked over 60 pints of beer.

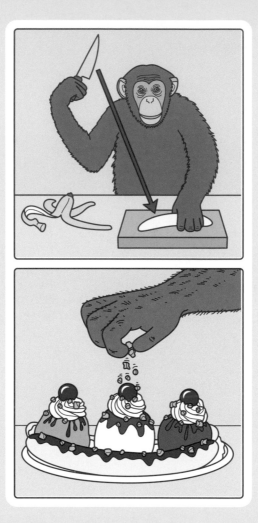

Banana Split

✔ Two bananas
✔ Vanilla, chocolate, and strawberry ice cream
✔ Chocolate, toffee, and strawberry sauce
✔ Crushed mixed nuts
✔ Whipped cream
✔ Glacé cherries
✔ Wafers

Too much booze seriously depletes the body of potassium and magnesium, both of which occur in bananas in decent quantities.

And the best way to wolf down bananas? The banana split, of course. Slice two bananas lengthwise down the middle and plop them on a plate leaving a small gap between them. Apply liberal scoops of vanilla, chocolate, and strawberry ice cream between the bananas. Douse the ice cream with chocolate, toffee, and strawberry sauce. Finally, garnish the lot with crushed nuts, whipped cream, and glacé cherries, then finish by stabbing the dessert with the wafers.

So easy, even a monkey could make it. Although he may struggle with crushing his nuts.

Milk Thistle Extract

✔ **Milk thistle extract**

This Mediterranean and Middle Eastern plant contains a substance known as silymarin. There's nothing silly about it—especially if you've been drinking heavily—since it greatly improves liver function and helps rid the body of alcohol's toxins.

The best way to take it on board is as milk thistle extract, a tablet, capsule, or liquid available from countless online pharmacies. Ideally, you should consume it before, during, and after your drinking session. But let's be realistic, you're hardly going to head to the bar with a bottle of the stuff in your pocket. Try it the morning after instead.

Liquid Legends

Painkillers were hard to find in the Wild West. You couldn't exactly pop to the nearest pharmacist. For cowboys, suffering after a long night at the local saloon sipping moonshine and playing poker, the answer was the dried droppings of jackrabbits, stirred into a cup of hot tea.

Meditation

The Buddhists aren't renowned for their binge-drinking habits. It's fair to say the Dalai Lama didn't get where he is today by spending his Saturday nights half cut on fermented yak's milk.

Nevertheless, many Buddhist chants have been known to alleviate the effects of even the worst hangover. This one, for example, which you should repeat seven times in a row, is supposed to cure your headache:

"Om nama sri padma hum kar ana thaya hara ka pa la vyat ham."

Should you choose to chant it on the train to work, however, you may get a few funny looks from fellow commuters. Much better to lie down in a quiet, candlelit room. Breathe in and out very deeply before you start the chant. In your mind's eye you should visualize your heart pumping nice, clean blood around your body, and your liver working efficiently to cleanse you of those nasty toxins.

Atholl Brose

- ✔ **Two parts Scotch whisky**
- ✔ **One part heavy (double) cream**
- ✔ **One teaspoon of clear honey**
- ✔ **Ice cubes**
- ✔ **One kilt and a pair of underpants (optional)**

According to legend, this hair-of-the-dog cocktail is named after the 1st Earl of Atholl, a rather crafty Scottish nobleman who quashed a Highland rebellion by spiking the rebel leader's water well with his special concoction.

Originally, the recipe called for oatmeal brose: water that has been soaked overnight in oatmeal and then strained through a muslin cloth. Since that requires a certain amount of forethought (which is always in short supply on boozy nights), it's a lot simpler to leave it out.

To make the easy version, mix all the liquid ingredients in a cocktail shaker with lots of ice. Shake vigorously to ensure the honey gets infused. Strain into a glass and knock it back. Preferably while wearing a kilt.

It works so well because the Scotch delivers you a hair-of-the-dog buzz, the cream takes the bite out of the Scotch, and the honey tops up your depleted sugar levels.

Liquid Legends

Nothing like a bit of Haitian Voodoo to rid yourself of a hangover. In the Caribbean, it's not unknown for drinkers to search desperately for the cork from the bottle of liquor that got them into trouble the night before. They then stick 13 black-headed pins into it. Works every time.

Bull's Penis Soup

✔ **One very angry bull**

The Bolivians like to cure hangovers and increase libido in one fell swoop. Their answer? *Caldo de cardan*, or bull's penis soup, which, they say, after a night of heavy boozing, perks you up in more ways than one.

And it's not some rare, high-priced delicacy. Wander round the restaurants of any Bolivian city on a Saturday morning and you'll spot loads of locals slurping the stuff. As well as the bull's genitalia, the soup also contains beef, chicken, lamb, boiled egg, rice, and potatoes.

It's obviously not for the faint-hearted. When you're nursing a headache and severe nausea, it's not always advisable to spoon a bull's most private parts into your mouth.

Borage

✔ **Ravioli or a bottle of Pimm's No. 1**

There's some documented scientific proof behind this one. In clinical trials, it was proved that *Borago officinalis*, a herb commonly known as borage, alleviates the worst effects of a hangover.

What wasn't scientifically proven was the best way to get the stuff into your system. It looks like you have two choices, depending on whether you fancy hair of the dog or not. You could either go Italian and eat a plate of ravioli, which is traditionally stuffed with borage. Or you could go British. They use borage to garnish a gin-based cocktail mix called Pimm's.

Liquid Legends

Here's a cure that's perfect for those hangovers where the thought of moving even a couple of feet fills you with dread. In some parts of Mexico, suffering señors and señoritas will lie in bed the morning after and pour a shot of tequila into their belly button. While they lie back and nurse their headache, the alcohol seeps slowly through the skin, into the bloodstream, hair-of-the-dog style.

Smoothie Overload

✔ **3½ oz (100g) of strawberries**

✔ **10½ oz (300g) of pineapple**

✔ **One large banana**

✔ **Juice of one lemon**

✔ **Ice**

Too much booze gives your body a serious spanking in the vitamin and nutrient department. So it's not surprising your body cries out for healthy food the morning after.

Fruit smoothies are the perfect answer, giving you a major injection of goodness, with just a minor amount of preparation. Try this one out for size. It's packed with vitamin C, magnesium, and potassium, all of which will have been depleted overnight.

Peel and chop up the strawberries, pineapple, and banana before throwing them into a blender with the lemon juice and a handful of ice cubes. Blitz the mixture for around 30 seconds until you have a smooth liquid, then pour into a glass, and enjoy as the nutrients in the fruit work their magic.

Eggnog

- ✔ **One medium free-range egg**
- ✔ **A measure of brandy**
- ✔ **A measure of dark rum**
- ✔ **One tablespoon of gomme syrup**
- ✔ **Three measures of milk**
- ✔ **Fresh nutmeg**
- ✔ **A Christmas tree**

If Santa Claus were ever the victim of a vicious hangover, this would surely be his favorite cure. It is perfect for those rather fuzzy Christmas Day mornings. (Not that Santa would ever imbibe too much, of course. No, not with all that sleigh-riding he has to do.)

Preparation is reassuringly simple. Mix the egg, brandy, rum, and gomme syrup in a cocktail shaker. Shake it all up as vigorously as your hangover allows. Strain it into a glass before stirring in the milk and grating the nutmeg on top.

Now for the scientific bit. The cysteine in the egg cleans up many of alcohol's poisonous effects, while the brandy and rum obviously do the opposite: they take the sting out of the hangover by giving you a hair of the dog.

Liquid Legends

Ancient Greeks and Romans may have been a civilised bunch, but when faced with a hangover they were forced to take desperate measures to cure their sore heads. In Rome they swore by deep-fried canaries and in Athens locals would sit down to a delicious breakfast of sheep's lungs. Definitely not the most appetizing of cures.

Acknowledgments

Thanks to all my fellow drinkers who, over the years, have (perhaps too) thoroughly tested many of these games with me that have caused many a hangover. Especially Sally, Jez, Naytin, Lucy, Oli, Weeve, Dave, Muzzer, Adam, Dom, Tash, Chaz, and Caz.